Dear Cancer, With love ...

Ian McGaffney

First published in 2020 by Paragon Publishing, Rothersthorpe

ISBN 978-1-78222-798-4

Book design, layout and production management by Into Print
www.intoprint.net
+44 (0)1604 832149

Receiving a diagnosis of cancer is in some way a life changing moment. It is one of those dates you never forget. It puts your life on hold, places everything in perspective, resets your priorities, and reminds you how fragile and precious life is. Everyone who experiences cancer assumes, suffers, and deals with it in their own personal way. This book recounts mine. In my case it morphed from purely dealing with a disease, to coexisting with it as if it were a personal relationship.

This book is dedicated to my wife, family, friends, medical staff, and others, who accompanied me on my journey in 2019. They are too numerous to mention, but they all know who they are. My appreciation and gratitude for their love and support is immense and would be difficult to be put into words. Suffice to say that I would not be here today if not for them.

Profits from the sale of this book will be donated by me to anti-cancer society *Asociación Española Contra el Cancer (AECC)*
e-mail: madrid@aecc.es

Ian McGaffney

With love …

Dear Cancer,

"There's a thin line between love and hate. Maybe you're confusing your emotions."

– SIMONE ELKELES, *Perfect Chemistry*

With love ...

Dear Cancer,

CANCER

Evil. Vile. Live.
Three words.
Four letters.
All the same.
They can become a sentence.
Or even define you.

Evil.
Is what you are.
Pure and simple.
It is in your nature.
Moves beyond the natural.
Becomes physical.
You are the devil reincarnated.

Vile.
Is what you do.
Working in the dark,
Silently.
Waiting.
Doing the devil's bidding.
You humiliate.
Contemptible and despicable.
Don't even come near.
Unpleasant is an understatement.
You leave a destructive trail wherever you go.

Live.
Inhabit if you will.
But you don't decide.
It's only temporary.
Accommodation.
Don't get used to it.
I prefer to live.
That's my decision.
Alone.
And to think.
Just one small change.
Could turn you.
Into love.

Dear Cancer,

SIGNS

I thought it was love
in the dark of the night,
a whisper in the ear.
Yet it felt like a hot needle,
woke me in fright,
announced you were near.

I thought it was drink,
a pain in the head
the very next day,
blinding my thoughts,
but hearing your words,
you were not going away.

I thought it was thirst,
maybe just a sore throat.
Impossible to swallow,
burning me inside.
It was only your way
of telling what was to follow.

Dear Cancer,

DIAGNOSIS

I hardly believed it,
told myself it's not true.
Tried to wish it away,
not knowing what to do.

I couldn't understand,
found it hard to relate.
Staring into an abyss,
could this be my fate?

You made it certain,
right from the start,
you were here to hurt me,
even break my heart.

I spoke to my God,
told him I'd make amends.
I tried to understand
the message He sends.

It's all very strange,
you start to embrace,
hold on with dear life,
to all that you face.

So how should I tell them
of your unwelcome visit?
A temporary arrangement?
Or what actually is it?

It was difficult at first.
Many tears were shed.
Whilst I thought of your presence,
constant in my head.

Coming to terms
with what lie ahead.
Explained by counsellors,
accustomed to dread.

They talked about you,
not at all flattering.
Whilst you lay dormant,
they would send you scattering.

They would stand up to you,
and you'd do as you were told.
Let me go forever,
and break your hold.

I'd pray to my God,
asking for care.
Then start realizing,
He'd always been there.

Dear Cancer,

THE "C"

Have you ever wondered
why they don't call you by name?
Yet they talk about you
all of the time.
Never anything good.
You must have hurt people,
their feelings and hopes.
They use so many words
to describe who you are.
So many different names
that amount to the same,
giving notice of your arrival,
a forewarning of suffering,
and harbinger of pain.

Dear Cancer,

NEGATION

The early days,
the sleepless nights,
I'd lie awake,
just me and my thoughts.
Not thinking of me,
only of those I'd leave behind.
Family, friends, and others
I'd no longer see.
Asking the questions,
convincing myself
It's not happening to me.
Clouds of sadness
rolling in,
tears of sorrow
raining down,
announcing the storm,
that is my tomorrow.

Dear Cancer,

CONVERSATIONS

I'd talk to myself,
also with others.
Friends and lovers,
sisters and brothers.

In the early hours,
all on my own,
asking myself questions,
the answers unknown.

I´d think about living,
not too far ahead.
Fearing to sleep
in case I wake up dead.

The thoughts would consume me,
prey on my mind.
The family would be there
to unravel the entwined.

The response is within me,
It´s just a matter of time,
until I reach the summit
after a difficult climb.

Dear Cancer,

YES, IT CAN HURT

Yes,
it can be a lonely place,
even though
you are surrounded
by many a familiar face.

It
can become a matter of time
against which you must race,
but it doesn't depend on you
who gets to set the pace.

Can
you really deal with it?
Does it ever take a break?
Does it give any respect,
to the life it wants to take?

Hurt
is what you're feeling.
In many a different way,
and yes, it can hurt those around you,
before it goes away…

Dear Cancer,

OTHERS

One actually thinks
it only happens to others.
You've already taken
my mother and brother.

One thing is certain,
you don't discriminate.
Young or old,
you don't hesitate.

You sometimes keep silent,
awaiting a date,
never showing your face
until sometimes too late.

You want to take hold,
increasing your grip,
not letting go,
not even a slip.

When your job's done,
nothing left to discover,
you take your leave,
move on to another.

Dear Cancer,

ATTITUDE

This is not about you.
It's about how I deal with you.
It comes down to choices,
all on my own.
Stop listening to voices.

Telling myself
you are not really true.
Looking for answers
of what I should do.

Let my demons loose,
at night in my head,
interrupting my dreams,
lying awake in my bed.

What I do with my life
is for me to decide.
I could always roll over,
find a place to hide.

I could just succumb,
give myself up to you,
blame only me,
assume what is due.

I could take the fight to you,
make you retreat.
Eliminate you forever.
No easy feat.

It´s all about
mind over matter.
If you don't mind,
it will eventually matter.

Dear Cancer,

THE MIND

The mind
can be a lonely place,
hiding fears
I don't want to face.

It can take control,
suggest the worse,
make me hungry,
or feed my thirst.

It changes my thoughts,
fuels my regret,
taints the future
awaiting ahead.

It strengthens its hold,
fills me with doubt
on how to proceed,
or find my way out.

It never rests,
nor stops to think
of the harm inflicted
reaching the brink.

It takes advantage of weakness,
dashes all hope,
paralyzes actions,
until unable to cope.

It's a place to conceal
the darkest thoughts,
hidden forever,
no matter how sought.

It takes over your head,
heart, body, and soul.
Weakens the spirit
whilst taking its toll.

Dear Cancer,

ATTENTION!

Sensation
Infection
Inflammation
Location
Question
Consultation
Investigation
Detection
Confirmation
Negation
Rejection
Oration
Revelation
Relation
Affection
Sedation
Radiation
Dehydration
Injection
Intention
Reduction
Redirection
Ejection
Termination
Prevention
Protection
Creation

Reflection
Redemption
Regeneration
Elation
Duration
Expectation
Determination.

Dear Cancer,

TREATMENT

You made my skin crawl
with your treatment of my neck.
The burning pain,
leaving me a wreck.

You lived off others
like a parasite,
whilst you built up your strength,
priming for a fight.

Every day,
though I could hardly stand,
you wanted to see me,
said you'd give me a hand.

Made me lie down,
dulled with CBD,
rolled into the darkness,
just you and me.

We listened together
to the endless whirring.
This was only for you,
but it left my blood stirring.

33 times, we met in the dark.
I could barely see, hardly breathe.
You didn't enjoy it,
it made you seethe.

It was for one of these reasons
you left me behind.
You could never understand
others being so kind.

You even drugged me.
Hour upon hour.
Making me sick for days after,
whilst exerting your power.

You made me lose weight,
not letting me eat.
Unable to chew,
my heart missed a beat.

Day after day,
week after week,
I saw my reflection.
The future looked bleak.

You stole my sleep,
poisoned my thoughts,
you just didn't care,
of the damage you wrought.

You interrupted my life,
filled my mind with hate.
I had to fight back,
before it was too late.

Dear Cancer,

My words dried up,
it was an effort to talk.
I would stagger to meet you,
almost unable to walk.

You left me weakened,
physically, mentally drained.
I wanted you gone,
even if the feelings remained.

We could live together
for quite some time.
I'd get to know your weaknesses,
whilst you'd get to know mine.

We might even love each other
in a very strange way.
If you treated me carefully,
I just might let you stay.

Or we could end up fighting
to the very end,
venting our hatred,
but that will depend.

You caused so much pain
to me and those nearest.
You couldn't care less
about all I held dearest.

You said that you loved me
whilst you sealed my fate.
The way you treated me,
I thought it was hate.

I wouldn't go with you,
nor wanted you to stay.
I was fighting you back,
turning you away.

I had the advantage,
I was not alone.
There were friends and family,
always there to atone.

We made you unwelcome,
made you feel it was all over.
You had no choice but to leave me,
your one-time lover.

So, for now I'm without you,
I continue to strive.
Its been too much time,
since I felt so alive.

You made me love to hate you
the more time that you stayed.
I ended hating to love you,
but I was no longer afraid.

Dear Cancer,

REFLECTION

I saw you every day
staring at me in the mirror.
The sunken eyes
in a hollow face.
The sagging skin
a shade of grey.
Traces of muscles.
Fading away.

You looked at me
like an empty soul,
thinking I would join you
on the other side
of the mirror.
I looked back defiant,
not understanding
what I had become,
but knowing for sure
I would not end like this.

I would see you change
in other visits.
A light in my eyes
growing stronger.
I would maintain my spirit,
stare you down,
accept you no longer.

Dear Cancer,

THE INVASION

You took over my life,
invaded my mind,
occupied my thoughts,
most of the time.

The nights were the worst,
giving me the darkest of thoughts,
when the devil would whisper
it's ok to give in.

You chose when I could sleep,
using patches against pain
and drugs for the head.
I'd wake up alive,
thinking
I was already dead.

Dear Cancer,

EARLY DAYS, LATE, LATE NIGHTS

I'd crawl to the water
doubled over by weakness
and unending fatigue.
Then dragged on my clothes
that hung from me like those of a clown.
Were they really mine?

And you stayed silent.
Just smiling,
Looking, laughing
at your unfinished work.

Carried away
to meet your victims
in God's waiting room.
Serene, with their empty stares
into an uncertain future.
Dealing their cards,
unsure of what hand they'd receive
or of what awaited beyond.

I'd lose my locks, looks and all.
The least of my problems
when the stakes are so high.
Back at the house,
the same old game.

Abundant food,
always too much.
Everything tried,
but like swallowing crushed glass.
Days after days with endless saliva
that eventually dried up,
leaving me gagging and heaving
on your vile green venom.

Loving hands would be there,
family and carers,
joining forces against you,
together in prayer.

I'd drift into darkness,
unwilling, unable to speak,
fearing closing my eyes
in case I'd see you
on the other side.

You thought this was permanent,
this assault on my spirit.
But my will was not broken.
I'd decided to deal with it.

Dear Cancer,

AWAITING RESULTS

Your visit was ending,
you'd wrecked all in the house,
left your host wounded,
you had to get out.

You left me reminders
that I'd keep for a while.
It was just as you planned it,
from the very first day.

You'd stolen my senses,
left little appetite for life.
Unable to swallow,
no taste for what's left.

You were still calling daily,
your tone in my ears.
Hard to ignore,
didn't allay my fears.

Then you left me thinking,
mostly on my own.
Awaiting to hear from you,
or news about you.

This uncertainty
almost as bad as your presence.
The waiting was killing me
all over again.

I was told you had left me,
but who knows for how long?
I, in the meantime,
had to make myself strong.

I've changed all the locks,
slammed shut every door.
I won`t let you back in.
I don't love you anymore.

Dear Cancer,

DOUBTS

Everyone said it was all over,
sometimes I feel that's not true.
No matter what they say,
at the end of the day,
it will just be me and you.

Maybe they're right,
I'm just dreaming at night,
thinking you're around,
without making a sound.

You're looking to enhance
what we already had.
You could never understand
why I wouldn't give you a chance.

You just wanted to fight,
to not let me go.
But I had to let you know:
I wanted you out of my sight.

Dear Cancer,

DOUBTING AGAIN

I'll tell you something
You'll try to return
Somehow
I feel it
Maybe you send a third party to visit
To try to harm me
And it confuses me
And that's your intention
Whatever happens
It will be your fault
And how long you remain
Only time can tell

Dear Cancer,

UNCERTAINTY

Sometimes
I fear
I'll find you
around another corner.
Waiting.
Hiding from me.
Getting ready
to pay me another visit.

You see how you make me
think about you?
You have this control
which is not healthy,
and at times keeps me awake.

Just so you know,
I've told my friends.
They are making sure I avoid you.
They don't want to see us
together again.
Ever.
You are not welcome around here.
I hope you get this message.

Dear Cancer,

UNFINISHED

If only you'd tried
just a little bit harder,
I wouldn't have lied,
we could have gone farther.

At the end of the day
it's better this way,
and now we both know
it was only for show.
So, what went on inside,
we don't have to hide.
How we made it to here,
we'll never know …

Alright, alright,
I could always stay all night,
and everything will be all right.
All you must do
is hold me tight.

Dear Cancer,

AFTER YOU LEFT

The constant ringing
in my head
made me only hear half
of all that was said.

I thought it was you
just calling to tell
that you were still around.
I hadn't broken your spell.

I still couldn't eat all
but certainly more,
and even tasting
what I couldn't before.

Gasping for air,
heaving the bile.
Nothing left inside,
just a feeling so vile.

So many dark thoughts
crept into my sleep.
Hid in the corners,
timing a leap.
Waiting to take over
at the first sign of weakness.

You can't let them in,
they will poison the mind,
take advantage
of whatever they find.

I promised my God,
I would make the amends.
Now I'm finally listening
to the message
He sends.

It's now up to me
to handle my fate,
take control of what's left,
before it's too late.

Once again
my clothes nearly fit.
Parts of my body returned
I could actually see it!

I´d waited for weight
to return to a frame.
Shrunken by sickness,
will never look the same.

At least I'm alive,
is all that I said,
knowing the alternative
was still in my head.

The occasional thoughts
were there to remind
you might return someday,
take what you left behind.

THERAPY

I searched for help,
a tender hand.
So many questions.
Try to understand.

It's all about life,
with not enough answers.
Coming to terms
with you and my cancer.

I say my prayers,
promise I'll change,
write the words down,
things can't stay the same.

I'm still alive
whilst others have gone.
So, don't ever complain.
Some have none.

It depends on you
as to how I will face
the healing processes
taking place.

They are there to help
on every visit.
Arrange your mind,
lift your spirit.

They touch the part,
make you bare all.
It might break your heart
if you start to fall.

It really does matter,
helps clear the mind.
When your life is in tatters,
they can be so kind.

Dear Cancer,

A LOVELESS RELATION - AN UNWANTED LOVE

In all the time we lived together
I rarely mentioned your name.
Why did I never write to you?
Maybe by not mentioning your name
I hoped you'd leave me alone.
Or maybe I just didn't want to admit
that you would only be with me until I tired of you
and cast you aside.
Whatever the outcome, it was never going to be an easy relationship.
We were always fighting each other.
You hurt me deeply, constantly, and silently,
causing me and my family pain and sorrow.
I had to realize that things had become personal,
that only one of us would survive unharmed.
Previously, the uncertainty would fill my thoughts
and I could not go on living like that.
Even though you might return,
I hope that you have left me forever …

Dear Cancer,

AN UNWELCOME VISITOR

Uninvited,
I barely saw you coming.
You moved in and took over
like you thought it was permanent.
You were a pain in the neck,
a real headache
that wouldn't leave me alone.

We shared some pain.
You hurt my feelings,
almost broke my heart,
but not my soul.
You changed my life,
but it's not yours to take charge.

So, I packed up my thoughts,
guarded my words,
recovered my dreams.
Opened my eyes,
and kept some images
as reminders of you.

I made up my mind.
So, take your leave.
Take all that's yours,
not missing a thing.
I'm not going with you.
I'm not ready to go.
Now am I clear?

Dear Cancer,

IS IT POSSIBLE?

So, you came back.
You're like a ghost
that follows me around.
God, did you not listen?
Didn't you get my message?
I never wanted to be found!

Now you are here,
what else can I say?
I feel you'll never leave me alone,
but haunt me all the time
until I finally give in.

Maybe you won't ever go away.

Dear Cancer,

AFTER WARDS

You remained there lurking,
waiting to pounce.
A surprising arrival,
unannounced.
You seemed so harmless,
yet made me fight for survival.

You took advantage of my distant stare.
What did you care?
You played on my fear,
took a piece of my life
every time you came near.

I thought you cared
when you touched my hair.
Whispered in my ear
though I could hardly hear.
Caressed my face
in a warm embrace.
Held me tight
throughout the night.

I don't ask much,
a hand, a touch.
A passing glance,
another chance,
maybe romance.
Even if only
our very last dance.

Dear Cancer,

AFTER ALL

You arrived uninvited,
interrupted my life.
You forced yourself upon me, even messed with my head.
I felt helpless
and I couldn't even help myself.
You fought with me constantly.
At times you made me suffer mentally,
physically, emotionally.
I wouldn't give up.
I didn't really want you
and you knew it … although I even proposed the counselling.
At least we stayed together a year
until I forced you to leave me.
This year I want to be alone.
I won't miss you.
I promise.
I might remember you sometimes, I can still feel you, hear you,
maybe even think about you.
I still don't want you back, ever!
Anyway, I never loved you
in any way.
Am I really clear?

About the Author

Ian was born on December 17th, 1951 in Liverpool, UK, and emigrated to South America in 1974 where he lived for over 40 years. A retired Company Director, he and his wife have been living in Madrid since 2016. He has three children and five grandchildren.

Ian was diagnosed with Cancer just before Christmas 2018 and started treatment early February the following year. It was only in January 2020 that he started to write of his experience, but from a different perspective. He invites you to accompany him on his journey via the preceding pages.

Dear Cancer, With love ... is Ian's first book in print, although he has been writing poems and musings since 1976, albeit for private consumption.

Initially, these poems were intended solely for family and friends, as before, but he was persuaded to publish to reach a wider readership, and so contribute in some small way to the ongoing research to find a cure for the disease.

www.ingramcontent.com/pod-product-compliance
Lightning Source LLC
Chambersburg PA
CBHW022125040426
42450CB00006B/846
* 9 7 8 1 7 8 2 2 2 7 9 8 4 *